Big Rigs

Quinn M. Arnold

CREATIVE EDUCATION • CREATIVE PAPERBACKS

seedlings

Published by Creative Education and Creative Paperbacks
P.O. Box 227, Mankato, Minnesota 56002
Creative Education and Creative Paperbacks
are imprints of The Creative Company
www.thecreativecompany.us

Design by Ellen Huber; Production by Joe Kahnke
Art direction by Rita Marshall
Printed in the United States of America

Photographs by Alamy (Joseph Sibilsky), Corbis (Jetta Productions/
Blend Images, Donald Johnston, David Nunuk/All Canada
Photos), Dreamstime (Andrew7726, Baloncici, Benkrut, Max
Blain, Alexandru Razvan Cofaru, Lougassi Gilles, Marchello74,
Tose, Luis Viegas, Vitpho), Flickr (maxually), Getty Images (Jetta
Productions), iStockphoto (Daniel Barnes, ryasick, StanRohrer),
Shutterstock (Robert Pernell, Michael Shake, Rob Wilson)

Library of Congress Cataloging-in-Publication Data
Arnold, Quinn M.
Big rigs / Quinn M. Arnold.
p. cm. — (Seedlings)
Includes bibliographical references and index.
Summary: A kindergarten-level introduction to the large
trucks known as big rigs, covering their purpose, drivers,
and such defining features as their tractors and trailers.
ISBN 978-1-60818-789-8 (hardcover)
ISBN 978-1-62832-385-6 (pbk)
ISBN 978-1-56660-819-0 (eBook)
This title has been submitted for
CIP processing under LCCN 2016937136.

CCSS: RI.K.1, 2, 3, 4, 5, 6, 7;
RI.1.1, 2, 3, 4, 5, 6, 7; RF.K.1, 3; RF.1.1

First Edition HC 9 8 7 6 5 4 3 2 1
First Edition PBK 9 8 7 6 5 4 3 2 1

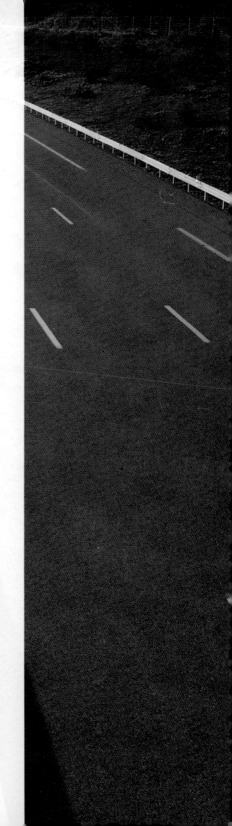

TABLE OF CONTENTS

Hello, big rigs!

Big rigs are large trucks. They drive on highways.

They carry heavy loads.

A big rig has two parts.

The front part is the tractor. This has the cab where the driver sits.

The back of a big
rig is the trailer.
It is very long.

The trailer carries the big rig's load.

Usually there is just one driver. But sometimes there are two.

Two people can take turns driving.

A big rig has 18 wheels! Ten wheels are on the tractor. Eight wheels are on the trailer.

They are in two groups of four.

Big rigs haul goods. They drive from city to city.

Goodbye, big rigs!

Picture a Big Rig

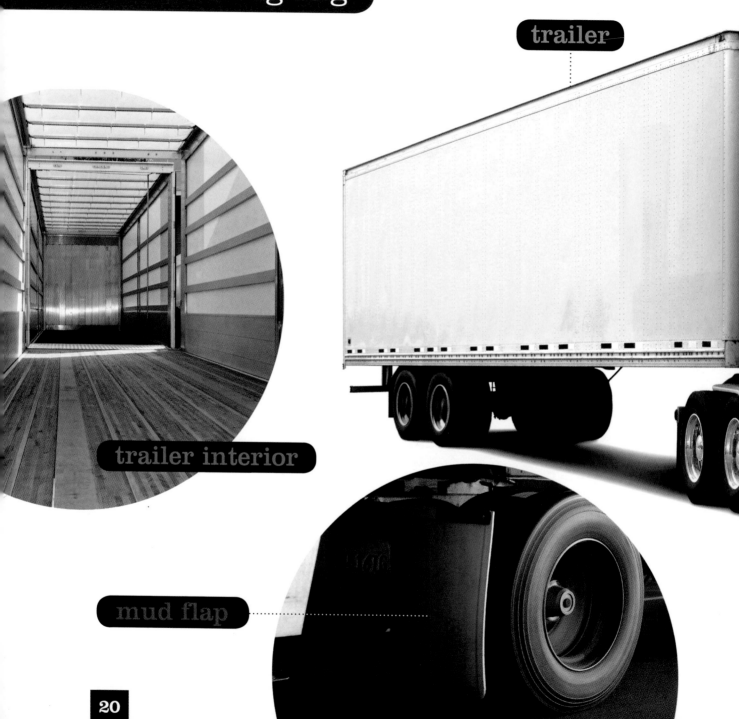

trailer

trailer interior

mud flap

exhaust pipe

horn

headlight

tractor

wheel

goods: things people can buy in a store, such as food, electronics, or clothing

highways: the main roads connecting cities

tractor: a short truck made up of a cab where the driver sits

Read More

Meister, Cari. *Big Rigs.*
Minneapolis: Jump!, 2014.

Nixon, James. *Trucks.*
Mankato, Minn.: Amicus, 2011.

Websites

Highlights Kids: Big-Rig Truck
https://www.highlightskids.com/crafts/big-rig-truck
Build your own big rig from recycled boxes.

Trucks Coloring Pages
http://www.coloring.ws/trucks.htm
Print out pictures of big rigs and other trucks to color.

Index